THE FUNNY SIDE OF
The Law

Stevenson Publications Limited

This book is published to help raise funds
for COMIC RELIEF and a donation of
10% will be made from every copy sold.

First published 1997

ISBN 0 9526395 9 9

Printed in Great Britain by
D. Brown & Sons Ltd, Bridgend.

Published by
Stevenson Publications Limited
19 Wharfdale Road, London N1 9SB.

THE FUNNY SIDE OF THE LAW

INTRODUCTION

A Community Officer in West Bar was determined to deliver a quality service to the elderly when he came to the aid of an old lady who appeared to be stranded in a heavy February snow fall. Our hero escorted the poor woman from the city centre to her home in Netherthorpe, battling on foot through ice and blizzard.
On reaching their destination however, his efforts went unappreciated. The pensioner, far from expressing gratitude on being rescued, said, "Now b****r off and leave me alone!"

Having played characters for so long who do all they can to avoid the law, I was quite surprised to be asked to write this introduction. But regardless of the book's theme, many of the stories, like the one above, are testament to what is special about the British sense of humour.
The fact that those who work in stressful and sometimes extremely dangerous conditions are so willing to share with us their less heroic and more embarrassing moments is a tribute in itself. And just as well too because without their contributions this book wouldn't have been possible. So here's to the girls and boys in blue. And here's to you too for buying this book and, in doing so, contributing to Comic Relief.

Cheers!   George Cole

George Cole

4

THE FUNNY SIDE OF THE LAW

English is said to be a complicated language. The following extracts from files and accident reports from Sheffield North Division show that it can have the best of us tied in knots...

Defendant: "That's falsely untrue, Sir."

Constable: "Did you hit him with the hand he bit you with?"

OSU Book: "No comment made, other than comments on pages 28 and 29."

Constable: "As I approached the bungalow, I saw a man mowing the lawn with a small child."

THE FUNNY SIDE OF THE LAW

Defendant: "I wouldn't say I was drunk, well the Officer who came and arrested me, he'd tell you I wasn't drunk." It was then established that the interviewing Officer *was* the arresting Officer.

Ex-Police Sergeant: "I am a retired police station."

Complainant: "I turned to face Martin who then head butted me in the nose area of my face."

An extract from a taped interview...
Constable: "Why did you drive off in the first place then?"
Reply: "I don't know, probably with me not having any licence."
Constable: "Right, I'm going to talk to you about that now. So you drove off because you'd got no driving licence."
Reply: "Yeah."
Constable: "You have no driving licence whatsoever?"
Reply: "No."
Constable: "No provisional licence?"
Reply: "No."
Constable: "So you've got no licence whatsoever?"
Reply: "No."
Constable: "Have you ever held a licence?"
Reply: "No."
Constable: "And obviously you've got no licence. Are you insured for the car?"
Reply: "No!"

'The complainant entered the chip shop and purchased a bag of chips. He was then battered by the defendant.'

6

'The defendant refused to give any explanation for his demise when arrested?'

'I looked at a young lady in shorts and the next thing I knew a lamp post jumped into my car.'

'I could recognise the defendant as I have known him for 15 years since he was 2 years old. He is my son.'

'The vehicles have all been positively identified as being stolen by the Doncaster Stolen Vehicle Squad.'

THE FUNNY SIDE OF THE LAW

Court in the act...

Question: "Now, Mrs Dixon, how was your first marriage terminated?"
Answer: "By death."
Question: "And by whose death was it terminated?"

Question: "Madam, were you cited in the accident?"
Answer: "Yes Sir, I was so cited I peed all over myself."

Question: "Do you drink when you're on duty?"
Answer: "I don't drink when I'm on duty, unless I come on duty drunk."

Question: "What is your name?"
Answer: "June McKenzie."
Question: "And what is your marital status?"
Answer: "Fair."

Question: "Are you married?"
Answer: "No, I'm divorced."
Question: "And what did your husband do before you divorced him?"
Answer: "A lot of things I didn't know about."

Question: "Officer, what led you to believe the defendant was under the influence?"
Answer: "Because, he was argumentary and he couldn't pronunciate his words."

THE FUNNY SIDE OF THE LAW

Question: "Did you ever stay all night with this man in Manchester?"
Answer: "I refuse to answer that question."
Question: "Did you ever stay all night with this man in Liverpool?"
Answer: "I refuse to answer that question."
Question: "Did you ever stay all night with this man in Blackpool?"
Answer: "No."

Question: "Were you acquainted with the defendant?"
Answer: "Yes, Sir."
Question: "Before or after he died?"

A Yorkshire regional newspaper published a story recently on vandalism in Barnsley which included:
'Passengers on a bus had a lucky escape when a bus was thrown through the window.'

THE FUNNY SIDE OF THE LAW

A Training Department Sergeant was enjoying his holiday walking along a Norfolk street when he heard a woman scream. He saw two men snatch her handbag and race from the scene. He set off in pursuit and floored the men. The local TV company were none too pleased at having to re-shoot the Crimestoppers version of the robbery.

A message went from Wombwell to Barnsley requesting inquiries to trace a missing girl by visiting 44 Park Street, 'the home of a friend, FNU SNU'. One and a half hours later, Barnsley replied: 'Park Street only goes up to 32. Electoral roll and telephone directory checked, no trace had any FNU SNU or anyone with surname SNU.' (Apparently the initials stand for forename unknown, surname unknown.)

An old stolen Ford Escort was found abandoned near Thorne and Scenes of Crime Officers were called to remove the number plates for fingerprinting. The Officers duly arrived at Thorne police station and espied a tatty Ford, which fitted the description given to them, parked in the Superintendent's bay. As they cut the plates off, one of the Officers remarked, "Who would steal a heap like that?" The observant duo took the plates back to Adwick for examination. Unfortunately, the number plates from the stolen car arrived at Thorne some 30 minutes later...the Specials Commandant was left with a car he could not drive!

11

THE FUNNY SIDE OF THE LAW

One enterprising Chief Superintendent decided to move from his office into the station library to hold a meeting with a visiting trade unionist to plan arrangements for an anti-pit closure demonstration. He took his visitor's coat and hung it in his office wardrobe. Shortly after entering the library, his secretary burst in to say that the wardrobe was on fire. The visitor had left his pipe smouldering in the pocket, totally destroying the coat. The Chief Superintendent's uniform hanging nearby was also badly charred.

In the Doncaster police station a harassed Custody Officer inquired if a prisoner brought to the counter was fit and healthy. "So your leg's not going to drop off then?" he asked. The prisoner and arresting Officer collapsed in fits of laughter and the latter eventually explained: "Sarge, he's got a false leg."

Extracts from A-Level Law exam papers...

'Drug addicts, ex-prisoners, insane people and the legal profession are exempted from the Jury system to safeguard the accused from injustices.'

'The Judge will require a unanimous verdict of 10-2.'

'The Jury has the advantage of being stepped in antiquity.'

'The Jurors are often said to be persons who can be found on the claphand buses.'

THE FUNNY SIDE OF THE LAW

When a man was stopped in Pitsmoor, Sheffield, without a tax disc, he had an explanatory note on his windscreen revealing that his tax disc had recently been seized by PC Jackson. He was, therefore, extraordinarily unlucky that the Officer who stopped him was none other than PC Jackson, who recalled seizing the disc not recently but a whole year before.

Two high-ranking German police Officers from Oberhausen in the Ruhr, accompanied by South Yorkshire colleagues, were visiting the Meadowhall Complex to pick up a few ideas on security as part of the planning for a similar mall in their area. A Security Officer invited them into the Conference Room to view the Meadowhall promotional video on an impressive large monitor.
Unfortunately, a member of staff had changed the cassette, and the D-Day landing sequence from the movie, The Longest Day flashed up on to the screen!

One Sheffield Wednesday supporter was clearly over the moon on his return from the drawn FA Cup Final at Wembley. Of the hundreds of vehicles returning from the pilgrimage to London, he singled out a coach full of South Yorkshire police staff to moon at from the front passenger window. No doubt he would have been sick as a parrot if anyone had waved a warrant card at him, but Officers saw the funny side and put it all behind them.

A suspicious package removed from a Sheffield house by the bomb squad turned out to be a personal vibrator!

A Constable on Attercliffe enquiry desk took a report of an accident from a man who was dyslexic. On reading the statement later, his Inspector noticed that the Officer had misspelt 'dyslexic'. When this was pointed out, the Constable replied, "I didn't know how to spell it, so I asked him."

A young Officer attended a burglary where the elderly occupant had been distracted by the offender who asked if he could get himself a glass of water and had left the tap running into the sink. The Officer advised the lady not to touch the tap until it had been examined for fingerprints by a Scenes of Crime Officer. Two days later the occupant telephoned Ecclesfield police station to ask when the SOCO might be arriving.

In response to the question in a road accident pro-forma statement: 'If any driver did not stop after the accident, did they appear to realise they had been in an accident? If so, give reasons.'
One witness replied: 'I think the driver realised he had been in an accident as his car was upside down in a field.'

A certain Superintendent and his wife were driving through France recently when they were stopped by the Gendarmerie for a random breath test. The French Officer stood in the middle of the road and was surprised when the lady refused to be breathalysed. She then pointed to the steering wheel, firmly in the grip of her husband, on the other side of the vehicle.

It must have felt like a belated April fool's joke for those who were caught out by the jingles promoting a local radio station's cash competition - a two-tone siren very similar to those used by the emergency services. Several drivers listening to Radio Hallam pulled in to let the phantom vehicle pass and they waited and waited. Among those sucked in was a presenter at Radio Hallam! Needless to say an Operations Room Inspector kindly suggested a juggle with the jingles.

The instruction to the Sheffield control room was to obtain a condition check after a police Officer was involved in a hit-and-run. A surprised Inspector was told: "I'm in the ambulance, I've got a headache and I think my leg's broken!"

15

THE FUNNY SIDE OF THE LAW

Officers manning calls for Crimestoppers started right from the bottom for the first of several special programmes. Instead of taking confidential calls about crime suspects the first bank of calls to the studios were from elderly woman asking how to solve irritable bowel syndrome!

Producer Ian Bevitt could not explain how calls meant for the 'Help Yourself' line got through but was clearly agitated. "The only person who had irritable bowel syndrome was me," he snapped.

A 'new broom' in the Chief Constable's office had been sweeping previously untouched corners. While tidying up the office in preparation for his work as the Chief's new Staff Officer, Inspector Graham Cassidy found a letter from a soldier asking to be considered for a job as a police Officer...dated 15 June 1907.

THE FUNNY SIDE OF THE LAW

A Sheffield Sergeant took his wife out for a romantic meal. At the restaurant, he remembered that a vital football match was being televised and 'phoned the baby-sitter to ask her to record it. When the couple returned they found that not only had the baby-sitter recorded the wrong programme, but had also recorded over their wedding video!

An Operations Room has perfected the art of being in two places at once - almost. Interviewed on radio following a fatal accident near a Rotherham canal, the Officer was asked to describe the scene. As he was standing outside Headquarters at the time, he decided to spare the reporter's blushes and improvise. Fortunately the nature of the questions required answers such as "dark", "murky", and "wet", but it was enough to fool his Chief Inspector who on hearing the broadcast on his way to work, demanded to know why one of his staff was in the middle of Rotherham and not behind his console!

Press Officers are often asked for information after being given the sketchiest of clues. Particularly vague was a request from a Sky News reporter after he attended a press conference at Heeley. Clearly harassed by an approaching deadline, he rang Headquarters minutes later to ask, "I've just spoken to a police Officer at the press conference and I forgot to get his name. Could you tell me who it was, please?"

THE FUNNY SIDE OF THE LAW

A shaggy dog story...

A Scottish couple had moved down South with their dog, Scooby. Sadly Scooby died and the couple decided to take him back to Scotland so they could bury him where he was happiest.

Scooby was wrapped in two duvet covers and laid on the back seat of the car for the journey North. Thinking it was illegal to bury pets in the open country, the owners decided to while away the afternoon in a local pub until it was dark. They had intended to ask an old friend who lived near Clydebank if they could bury Scooby on his land but when they arrived at the house there was no answer so they returned to the pub to wait. After several return journeys (and many drinks) the couple decided that their friend must be away so they made their way to Old Kirkpatrick to bury Scooby there.

By this time the man was almost legless but, having found a suitable slip-road leading to the old canal, they parked and he started to dig the grave. Almost immediately things started to go wrong. The man developed a severe nose-bleed, simultaneously suffered a small epileptic fit and collapsed. Panicking, the lady ran to the main road and flagged down a passing taxi driver who contacted the emergency services.

Rushing back to the scene, the lady hurriedly tried to hide all evidence of the intended burial; she hid poor Scooby under a sheet of polythene and threw the two heavily bloodstained duvets over a low wall at the side of the road.

The couple were taken by ambulance to the hospital where, after treatment, they were released and transported back to Old Kirkpatrick to collect their car. The Police were satisfied that the couple had merely looked for a quiet spot for privacy, and as far as they were concerned the matter was closed.

The couple drove back to their friend's house, parked up and spent the rest of the night asleep in the car.

At 09:00 the following morning two officers on early shift decided to drive down the canal road on their rounds. Knowing nothing of the previous evening's excitement they were naturally alarmed to discover the bloodstained duvets lying in the undergrowth. Closer inspection revealed vast quantities of blood on the road surface, grass and bushes.

They called the control room who in turn contacted the CID and before long several officers were at the scene. The force helicopter was summoned to search the area for possible heat sources and the area was cordoned off awaiting the arrival of forensics. Meanwhile door to door enquiries were underway.

By 11:00 details of the nose-bleed incident were found and the couple were eventually traced. Full statements were obtained, blood samples taken and all evidence, including photographs, duvets and dog collar were collected.

The whole incident was neatly tidied up - by about four o'clock that day.

THE FUNNY SIDE OF THE LAW

Rotherham Officers contacted the Operations Room and got a telephone number for a Bosnian interpreter. On dialling they heard, "University of Sheffield Bisexual Helpline, how can I assist?"

A lady motorist had broken down on the M4. The operator on the motorway console asked, "Which side of the motorway box is your vehicle?" (meaning east or west of the box). To this the lady answered after some thought, "The passenger side."

An operator received a 999 call regarding a man lying unconscious on a street in Blaenavon. The operator immediately passed the call on to a Police Constable in the area who replied, "Yeah, I've just driven past him. I'll go back now."

A telephone caller had clearly got the wrong number when he rang the Press Office at Police Headquarters and asked, "Is that the plumber?" "Sorry, no," came the reply, "but we're used to dealing with leaks and taps."

"Can't talk, Reg, the old bill have tapped the phone."

'Observations were made for a male aged in his 40's, 5' 2",
wearing blue tracksuit bottoms, green top, grey hair and
full beard, responsible for a sexual assault on a bus.'

*A West Bar Community Officer was determined to deliver a
quality service to an elderly citizen, whether she wanted it
or not. The knight in shining armour came to the aid of an
old lady who appeared to be stranded in a heavy February
snowfall. Our hero escorted the unhappy woman from the
city centre to her home in Netherthorpe, battling on foot
through ice and blizzard. On reaching their destination,
however, his efforts were unappreciated. The pensioner, far
from expressing gratitude on being rescued said, "Now
b****r off and leave me alone!"*

"Whose turn is it to clean out the hamster cage?"

Whilst his wife and daughter were out, an Inspector decided to do them a favour by cleaning out the hamster's cage. As soon as he removed the lid, the animal sank it's teeth into his index finger and steadfastly refused to let go even as it's fur became covered in blood. On finally shaking it loose, he was horrified to see it fall to the carpet whereupon his dog tried to pounce on it. The hamster scurried under furniture to safety. After controlling the dog the Inspector picked up the hamster which repaid his kindness by sinking it's teeth into his other index finger. More blood flowed as he struggled to free himself. Several days later, whilst mending his letter box which had stuck, his dog saw his fingers wiggling through the hole and bit them.

THE FUNNY SIDE OF THE LAW

Taking down a few particulars...

'At 14:35 Detective Constable B arrested the below-named for burglary at the ...... club. Method - cut phone wire, entered building, stole cash and property value £1000 and then left an uncomplimentary note for Detective Constable W which immediately identified the defendant.'

'At 21:45 Police Constable M arrested the below-named for disorder. Circumstances - Gestured at Officer with his finger who (sic) when spoken to became abusive, using obscene language.'

An extract from General Orders number 27, concerning Corporate Development briefing seminars reads... 'To reach as many people as possible and reduce demand on our staff, we feel that *afternoon* briefing sessions are the most effective way of sharing information. Bear that in mind, if you wish to attend the next session which will be held in the Lecture Theatre at Headquarters at 10*am* on Friday 23 July.'

An ex-footballer, now on the community beat in Hackenthorpe, innocently posed for a photograph for the Star newspaper to promote a local open day. Unfortunately the picture was placed directly under the headline of a neighbouring article which screamed...
'Bogus Officer in Sex Attack.'

THE FUNNY SIDE OF THE LAW

A few years ago I was on duty on the front desk when a member of the public brought in a black labrador dog that they had found sitting on the steps of the Shire Hall council building. I entered the details in the 'found dog' book and put the dog in the outdoor kennels.
A little later on I saw a similar dog walking past the window. The dog had escaped! I was obviously very concerned and although I looked for it, it was nowhere to be found.
One of the 'old sweats' in the station said, "Don't worry, I'll sign the book to say it was mine and that I've taken it home."
I took him up on his offer and thought that was the end of it until an hour or so later when a female council worker came in and said "I understand you have got my black labrador dog here."

A recently commended probationer Constable attended the scene of a possible burglary with colleagues and volunteered to climb up and through a suspiciously ajar window. All was in order and at that moment the young householders returned and explained that they had been decorating and had left the window open to let the paint dry. The new stripes on the young Constable's uniform apparently looked very fetching.

Traffic Warden's report...
'Gentleman moved his vehicle after I pointed out the offence to him. He was collecting stationary (sic).'

THE FUNNY SIDE OF THE LAW

A couple of years or so ago I was on duty in the Leamington control room on a busy Friday night when the 'phone rang and a lady from the most well to do area of the town asked me if we would be patrolling her area that night. I replied that I expected we would, providing that we weren't too busy. She then said, "Well when you are passing, could one of your Officers drop me in 20 Benson and Hedges and I will pay them next week?"

Operations Room staff were puzzled as to the source of a technical fault which had wiped out a message link to all other forces in the country. Computer staff spent many hours trying to find the fault, which was eventually traced to the terminal interface in the telex room. As there was no out-of-hours contact numbers for the service engineers, the force telephone expert was called. He tried to reset the system, but to no avail. Operations Room staff with some knowledge also tried to reset the interface using a manual for guidance. No luck. Eventually the engineers from Bradford were called and attended 36 hours later. Two men arrived, entered the telex room, removed a cable from a port at the rear of the interface and inserted it into the only other one available. The job took a couple of minutes.

Two letters received from Irate Citizens read...
'All this time Police Constable B, whom I believe to be a mute, did not say anything.' and, 'The people of Birmingham who are concerned for justice will step up their campaign under the slogan Fight Crime Disband The Police.' Oh well. You can't please all of the people all of the time!

THE FUNNY SIDE OF THE LAW

The custody Officer was busy in the cell block when the control room got an irate call from a man complaining about the cold and asking if he could have an extra blanket. Thinking that 'we had a right one here' he was asked where he was calling from and it turned out that he was a prisoner using the custody Sergeant's pre-programmed mobile 'phone which he had inadvertently left in the cell.

One summer on night traffic patrol duties my colleague and I came across a car we believed to have been involved in a recent smash and grab. Sure enough a chase ensued through town and country for about 20 miles at speed and with the target car driving very dangerously.
The villains were disposing of the booty, hundreds of packets of cigarettes, out of the window as they went. It became clear that there was no way they were going to shake us off, but on it went. Imagine our surprise then, when after all this time, the target car returned to the town, went along the police station road, down the station drive and around the back, pulling up neatly outside the 'tradesman's entrance' to the cells before putting their hands up!

Waiting impatiently for the press to appear for a photocall, a Senior Officer became a little confused in his excitement at spotting a camera crew. "They're here at last," he announced authoritatively, "I've just spotted the boom." The window cleaner standing clutching his mop grabbed his bucket and made a run for it.

Question: "Doctor, did you say he was shot in the wood?"
Answer: "No, I said he was shot in the lumbar region."

Question: *"And what did he do then?"*
Answer: *"He came home and the next morning he was dead."*
Question: *"So when he woke up the next morning he was dead?"*

The early 1970's saw the entrance to the police service of many miners from the Yorkshire area. One of them, known as the 'Underground Savage' soon found himself in the Magistrates Court giving evidence against a man he had arrested for shoplifting and for being drunk and disorderly. The defendant had pleaded guilty to shoplifting but disputed the charge of drunkenness. He was represented by an eloquent local Solicitor who was engaged in quite a lengthy cross-examination of the police Officer.

"My client admits he may have had a half pint of lager that afternoon, Officer, but he most certainly was not drunk."

The Officer was giving evidence from his notebook. "I saw him at 3:30pm on High Street, he was unsteady on his feet, his eyes were glazed, his speech was slurred, he was waving his arms about and he was clearly drunk."

"I put it to you Officer, he was not drunk. You may have seen him come from licensed premises, but he was not drunk."

Again the Officer read from his notebook. "I saw him at 3:30pm on High Street, he was unsteady on his feet, his eyes were glazed, his speech was slurred, he was waving his arms about and..."

The Solicitor interrupted. "Yes Officer, we've heard, but again I put it to you that my client was in no way drunk, nor was he disorderly."

The Officer looked up to the Magistrates and said, "If he weren't drunk, I want a couple of them tablets he's taking."

Prosecution: "Do you know how far pregnant you are right now?"
Answer: "I will be three months on September 10th."
Prosecution: "Apparently then, the date of conception was June 10th."
Answer: "Yes."
Prosecution: "What were you and your husband doing at the time?"

Prosecution: *"How did you happen to go to Dr. Wilson?"*
Answer: *"Well, a lady down the road had had several of her children by Dr. Wilson, and said he was really good."*

Prosecution: "The truth of the matter is that you were not an unbiased, objective witness, isn't it? You too were shot in the ordeal?"
Answer: "No, Sir. I was shot midway between the ordeal and the navel."

Prosecution: *(Showing man's picture)* *"That's you?"*
Answer: *"Yes Sir."*
Prosecution: *"And you were present when the picture was taken?"*

Prosecution: "Doctor, what is the meaning of sperm being present?"
Answer: "It indicates intercourse."
Prosecution: "Male sperm?"
Answer: "That is the only kind I know."

Question: "Was that the same nose you broke as a child?"

A well known High Court Judge was sentencing a burglar - "Jones". Jones thought he was going to get a two year sentence, but the Judge had other ideas and sentenced him to four years.

As the Jailer was taking Jones away to start his stretch, Jones said, "That old w****r."

Now the Judge had perfect hearing, heard this and told the Jailer to bring Jones back.

"That will be another six months for contempt!" said the Judge to Jones. With Jones in the dock and looking sheepish the Judge said to him, "Jones. When I leave this place of justice tonight, I will go home to my house which backs on to the River Thames. I will be greeted at the door by my dear wife, who will then pour me a Gin & Tonic, which I will take into the garden until my evening meal is ready, which I believe is pheasant with all the trimmings. With that meal we will open and share a good bottle of wine. After our meal we will retire to our drawing room, where I will have another Gin & Tonic and light up one of my favourite cigars then listen to the best classical music before retiring to my bed. Whereas you, Jones, are going to Wormwood scrubs. So who is the w****r, now? Take him away."

Whilst still a young probationer I was called to an old folks home because staff were concerned for an old lady they could not raise. They had the keys to the flat but the door was bolted from the inside and there was no response. Fearing the worst I smashed a window with my truncheon and went in. In the bedroom the old dear lay on the bed, ashen coloured and stone cold; shaking and shouting brought no response and I could not find a pulse. Saddened, I returned to the front door and let the two wardens inside. I had just broken the bad news to them when I saw a puzzled expression on their faces, I turned and nearly collapsed myself when I saw the little old 'dead' lady standing behind me.

THE FUNNY SIDE OF THE LAW

As a young Royal Military Police Second Lieutenant in Edinburgh in the mid 1960's, it fell to me to run the Absentees and Deserters (A & D) section.

On a Thursday one of the local highland battalions returned from Aden after a six month unaccompanied tour. After a days shakedown the troops were given until the following Monday evening to revisit their families. Experience told us that many would not return on time, so we deployed several A & D teams on the Tuesday, throughout Scotland, to round up the offenders.

In one tenement block in Glasgow I knocked on a door to be greeted by the most immediately dressed young jock, resplendent in kilt, tunic and bonnet, who immediately surrendered himself to me. On our trip back I asked him why he was late back, as he did not fit the description of the typical AWOL.

"Well Sir," he said, "It's like this; when I got back on Friday the wife was in the bath and it takes three days for a kilt to dry!"

A call to his CO ensured that he was dealt with leniently.

THE FUNNY SIDE OF THE LAW

The following extracts appeared in A-Level Law exam papers...

'Sometimes they don't send the criminal to prison but to a maintle people hosptile so that they can fix there his damaged brain from bad to good.'

'Sometimes if Judges apply the literal rule it could result in a wrong decision being made. If they think this is likely they can apply the golden or mischief rule and I cannot remember what either of them are so I will not waffle on.'

'It is not always necessary to involve the legal profession. Such disputes as those with the Inland Revenue can be solved by payment of the said amount. This is an equitable remedy.'

'If the job (gathering evidence) was done by Solicitors themselves, legal executives will probably cease to exist. But they do exist and get paid for their work.'

'The Ejusdem Generis rule:
For example an Act may say that no dogs, cats, hamsters are allowed in a certain place. This also means that no camels, elephants or giraffes are allowed either. Judges must watch carefully for cases involving acts like that.'

'Certain people are not allowed to sit in the Jury as this might form a biased opinion such as a clergyman or a renowned criminal.'

"Shove off! This is my patch!"

Control room log: Woman caller - "I saw a naked man behind a tree yesterday. I shall be there after 8pm tonight."

THE FUNNY SIDE OF THE LAW

An operator took a 999 call. The caller said, "A man has come into our house and hit my husband in the face!" The operator then replied, "Do you know this man?" The caller answered, "Yes, of course I do, he's my husband."

Conversation between the Force Control Room Inspector and operator...
"That stabbing - is it in hand?"
"No, Sir. It was in the neck."

An operator received a radio message from an Officer regarding three shoplifters walking towards the Tutshill area. The only description he had was, "One female with ginger hair accompanied by two males, no description." Tutshill police were contacted and the description was passed on as "One female with two ginger heads."

An operator was attempting to establish if an Officer was still at an incident so she asked over the radio, "Are you all there?" To which he replied, "Yes, thank you."

Detective Inspector Kevin Hardy of Attercliffe Police Station, Sheffield, was scanning the Detective Inspector's briefing sheet for the morning and noticed four undetected shoplifting offences. When he queried this with the Crime Management Sergeant, Mike Savory, Mike said: "Yes, it's PC World."
DI Hardy replied: "Well he wants speaking to!"
"No," said Mike, "PC World - the new computer shop!"

Caller to operator: "There is a car blocking my back passage. Can an Officer come and have a look please? I can't get things in and out. It has been there for some time."

Being short of funds our force asked a colleague and myself if we would be prepared to work over for time off in order to take a juvenile remand prisoner to a neighbouring county's remand centre.

Happy to oblige, we took the juvenile handcuffed in the back of our vehicle and left him at the centre's reception before leaving at a great rate of knots, wondering what we would do with the time off we had just earned. We hadn't quite reached home when we got a call on the radio asking us if we could return to the centre and remove the prisoners handcuffs as they hadn't got a key.

I was the observer in an area response car one night when we were chasing a stolen vehicle. After a couple of miles the stolen car turned into a cul-de-sac and stopped at the end, the occupants making a run for it.

Being as keen as mustard I wanted to continue to chase on foot. I estimated the speed of our vehicle, wrongly, to be about running pace when I unbuckled and began to get out of the car to run after them. Sadly I learnt later it was nearer 20 mph when I got out and tried to run. Predictably I began to fall whilst still holding on to the door, was dragged along for 20 yards when my legs spun around and I watched the rear nearside wheel of our car drive straight over my right thigh. I still managed to join the driver in a foot pursuit of the villains.

At the end of last year myself and another Officer, both getting on in service, were put back on the beat having spent years in the control room. We were keen to show the shift that we still had 'what it takes', so when we were crewed up together in an area car we made sure we had all the kit that we were likely to need, including a breathalyser kit. Later on the first night we had occasion to stop a car and require the driver to take a breath test. Unfortunately my colleague couldn't find the kit, cursing the rest of the shift. Assuming that one of them had taken our kit we had to call up for a car from the next town to bring us a spare kit. It was only when we got back in the police car did we realise that my colleague had been sitting on it all the time.

Motorist reported for using a car without licence, tax or test certificate replied...
"I wouldn't have used it but the television dropped on the baby's head."

Application form completed on a potential Special Constable, under 'Marks, disfigurements' the Sergeant recorded - 'Visible love bites on neck.'

Appraisal report on probationary Constable...
'The question of her apparent dislike of walking her beat was raised but it turns out she had a period when her feet were very tender and in need of care. She is now treating her feet so performance should improve.'

Appraisal...
'Another matter discussed with her was her brusque manner when speaking to members of the public who approach her. This she puts down to her training in her previous job with the DHSS.'

Probationer suggested a summons for 'Provisional licence holder driving a motor vehicle on a road whilst unoccupied.'

'I walked into the wood, a distance of 150 yards out of sight of the main road, where I saw my car. It was on it's side. It was in a bad state, many parts including the engine, wheels, tyres, petrol tank and radio cassette had been removed, just leaving the basic chassis and shell behind. The vehicle was totally undriveable.'

38

THE FUNNY SIDE OF THE LAW

Extract from Police report...
'Police Constable S was driving police vehicle in Folly Road, turned right into the car park. The vehicle passed over a sleeping policeman.'

Witness questionnaire...
Question: State position and movement of pedestrian - Before the accident: 'Upright'.
After the accident: 'Lying by the kerb.'

Operator on motorway console answering motorway 'phone to lady who was ringing back: "Are you a blue Sherpa?"

'The defendant continued to struggle and I drove to Hammerton Road Police Station, threatening both the licensee and myself with physical violence.'

Constable's report: 'I attended at 26 Mayfield Road where he had been bitten by a dig.'

A colleague asked me to send a unit to a house in Warwick. Apparently a lady's dog was going mad and wouldn't stop barking as there was a sea lion in her front garden. When the Officer arrived and asked where the sea lion was, the woman became rather nasty and replied, "What sea lion, I said feline!"
I still can't work out why she called us in the first place.

An applicant for the force wrote...
'In 1983 I won a national essay writting competition.'

Motorist pleading for leniency after receiving a parking ticket...
'I am writting (sic) to you, hopping (sic) that you will believe me and consider my case like those where someone is feeling that he is telling the truth but he can't prove it.'

From motorist's statement...
'I want to tell that parking on the roof of this shopping centre is the cheapest...'

Another motorist's statement...
'If you would bare (sic) with me a moment I would like to tell you the reason for parking there and being fined.'

The problems of decision making can be highlighted when considering the following accident report...
'The driver of vehicle 2 alleges that vehicle 3 stopped over the give-way line at it's junction and that vehicle 3 was to blame for the accident. The driver of vehicle 3 blames the driver of vehicle 1 for the accident stating that vehicle 1 was being driven at excessive speed. The driver of vehicle 1 blames the drivers of vehicles 2 and 3, stating that they emerged in front of him.'

There used to be a very large mental hospital on my old patch just outside Warwick and I was always getting called there for various reasons. One day I was flagged down by a very worried man who insisted that the staff were trying to kill him. I asked him how long this had been going on and he replied, "Twenty five years."

41

THE FUNNY SIDE OF THE LAW

Friday Night, 22nd November 1996...

My attention was drawn to a panda in the High Street of the town I was patrolling. The staggering creature appeared to be stopping the traffic, causing much inconvenience to motorists.

The panda was approached, with caution, by myself and the WPC I was with, when we noticed the famous BBC Children In Need Pudsy Bear logo on a bucket it was holding. We told the panda that we appreciated the good intentions of collecting money for charity but we pointed out that he was liable to arrest and would be placed in a Panda car and taken to the station, if he caused any further trouble.

An hour or so later myself and my colleague saw the same, now very intoxicated, Panda brawling outside a local fast food take-away in the same street. In short he was arrested for Drunk and Disorderly and conveyed to the police station.

Upon arrival the panda became awkward and was not too happy. He said that we were doing the wrong thing as he was only collecting money for Children In Need. Trying to humour him, we pointed out that pandas were an endangered species and that we may be doing him a favour by taking him into protective custody.

Having presented the panda to the custody Sergeant in the normal fashion (as you do with wild animals), Panda refused to give his name. Panda said that he wanted to speak to his partner who we managed to trace at the front desk, dressed as a Lion. We asked Lion for Panda's name to which the reply was "F**k off!"

Solicitor's letter...
'Whilst we view these instructions with some scepticism we cannot believe that 14 police Officers would attend the house of a 45 year old woman merely to arrest her for non-payment of fines.'

THE FUNNY SIDE OF THE LAW

Sergeant appraising a Constable...
'This Officer has a large police experience.'

Police appraisal...
'This Officer has been moved stations after 19 years following a minor discretion.'

Question in Court: "What happened then?"
Answer: "He told me, 'I have to kill you because you can identify me."
Question: "Did he kill you?"
Answer: "No."

Question in Court: "Doctor, how many autopsies have you performed on dead people?"
Answer: "All my autopsies have been performed on dead people."

"That was close, I almost spoilt my record."

THE FUNNY SIDE OF THE LAW

USA Court extracts...

Question: "Mrs Williams, is your appearance this morning pursuant to a deposition notice which I sent to your attorney?"
Answer: "No. This is how I dress when I go to work."

Question: "And lastly, Tommy, all your responses must be oral, OK? What school did you go to?"
Answer: "Oral."
Question: "How old are you?"
Answer: "Oral."

Question: "What is your relationship with the plaintiff?"
Answer: "She is my daughter."
Question: "Was she your daughter on March 12th 1982?"

Prosecution: "Now, you have investigated other murders, have you not, where there was a victim?"

Question: "Did he pick the dog up by the ears?"
Witness: "No."
Question: "What was he doing with the dog's ears?"
Witness: "Picking them up in the air."
Question: "Where was the dog at the time?"
Witness: "Attached to the ears."

Question: "Did you tell your lawyer that your husband had offered you indignits?"
Answer: "He didn't offer me nothing, he just said I could have the furniture."

THE FUNNY SIDE OF THE LAW

A dog handler was giving evidence at the Magistrates Court having arrested a man for being drunk and disorderly. Outlining the circumstances leading up to the arrest, he was describing the defendant's conduct and language.

"At this stage," he told the Magistrates, "he said, if you don't go away, I'll kick your f*****g dog!"

"Then what happened?" asked the Chairman of the bench.

"He kicked my f*****g dog!" came the reply.

On 22nd December 1996, a hapless traffic patrol Officer was driving along the M25 motorway in Berkshire, when she spotted a broken down Volkswagon camper van on the hard shoulder. She stopped to help the stranded occupants who consisted of five young children, their mother and grandmother.

During the course of conversation, and in the process of arranging recovery for the vehicle, the children's mother asked the WPC to speak to her five year old son who was refusing to wear his seatbelt. Always willing to help, the Officer berated the child at some lengths about the dangers of not wearing a seatbelt. This, however, was clearly not working so in one final attempt the Officer told the child, "If you don't wear your seatbelt, Father Christmas won't bring you any presents."

This appeared to have the desired effect as the child promptly started crying, and put on the offending seatbelt. The Officers pride was quickly turned to embarrassment when the child's grandmother said, "He won't be getting any presents anyway. We're all Jehova's Witnesses!"

THE FUNNY SIDE OF THE LAW

More A-Level law exam papers....

'Capital punishment is seen as being one of the greatest deterrences of all.'

'Deterrence probably works if the person is reconvicted for a different offence. If the same offence, then it has not worked.'

'Retribution is where you sentence the criminal because he deserves it e.g. - sentencing a murderer to life imprisonment because that's what murderers get.'

'Taking a case to court will cost a lump.'

"It's to cover my legal fees."

THE FUNNY SIDE OF THE LAW

Solicitor's letter dealing with a civil claim against the police...
'We are prepared to conceive by all means...'

Police appraisal report...
'He has shown the ability to adjust well to the change of pace and roll (sic).'

WPC reported the below named for section 47 assault using a crutch...
'Robert Neil Foot.'

Police appraisal...
PC when asked what he saw as his weaknesses wrote, 'My English and writting still requires improvement.'

Complainant wrote...
'Having been a member of the Green Party I am wondering if this search had a political motif .'

From Police appraisal...
'I supervised Police Constable B on an ad hock basis.'

Taken from law exam paper... 'With the tort of negligence the rule of *Rylands Fletcher* applies. It states that where a person has on his property a dangerous thing or substance he is liable to his neighbours for the escape of it. We then ask who then in law is my neighbour. The answer implies that anyone who is closely will be affected by my act that I ought reasonably to avoid.'

THE FUNNY SIDE OF THE LAW

A few years ago, on a cold and windswept winter night, I attended the scene of a burglary on the Parson Cross Estate, Sheffield. The rain was lashing down and, as I approached the front door of the house, I saw in the darkness a small mongrel dog whimpering and pawing at the door.
A little old lady answered the door and, as I stood introducing myself, the dog went in and made itself comfortable in front of the fire. Whilst upstairs carrying out my fingerprint examination, I commented on what a friendly little dog she'd got and remarked on what good company it must be for her.
What she said almost brought on a panic attack. "Nay lad, it's not me dog. A've never seen it before in me life, in fact I thought it'd come with thee and were a police dog."
Realising I had made a wrong assumption, I offered to remove the dog. Sensing my approach, the nice little dog had now turned into a snarling wide-eyed beast. After much pulling and tugging, I managed to get it outside where, after registering it's displeasure by trying to bite me, it disappeared into the night never to be seen again.

Prostitute to police Officer arresting her...
"Just take me in, I'll plead quilty. You are a big ugly bastard though."

How about this for a pen picture by a Superintendent of a Sergeant...
'His solemn mien and considerable gravitas often give the impression of a humourless functionary.'

49

PC Warnes and WPC Graham were on uniformed mobile patrol in Farnborough, Hampshire, when they responded to a call for assistance from detectives who had arrested a man for possessing drugs. On arrival PC Warnes got out of the car and went to assist the other Officers. As he handcuffed the prisoner and walked him back to the car he saw that WPC Graham had not left the car and the interior appeared to be full of smoke. On arriving back at the car PC Warnes asked WPC Graham what had gone on to be told he had stepped on the fire extinguisher as he got out of the car.

Finding this extremely funny he loaded the prisoner and got back into the car and on closing his door stepped on the fire extinguisher again covering all occupants in dry powder. The prisoner was not impressed.

Letter from Solicitors regarding their client who alleged assault...

'We understand the police were called, but during the following week when we attempted to discover what action would be taken we were told your computer had broken down. We feel that we should point out that although Mr A is the father of Mrs H's youngest child, there had never been co-habitation. Nor is Mr A welcomed at Mrs H's flat. Therefore the situation is little different from a common assault on a stranger and certainly not just a domestic dispute."

Report by police Officer on a disturbance in a public house...

'On arrival I saw a barmaid, Mrs Elizabeth Jones, 80 years.'

Special course candidate at interview when asked about equal opportunities confided...
'I've studied a few policewoman on my shift for the promotion exam.'
The same candidate also wrote that he was involved in 'Life Safeing.'

Another candidate revealed...'Other mild punishments such as parole and bail are allowed.'

"If you're really bad I can hit you with a baloon on a stick."

THE FUNNY SIDE OF THE LAW

On Wednesday 7th June 1995, PC Bluestone and Forsyth were on early turn in the Dartford response car. It had been a relatively boring day and they were on their way back to Dartford from Swanley. The route took them along the A20 towards the M25. This location is also known as the Swanley Interchange and there are several sets of traffic lights controlling the various roads.

A few hundred yards in front of their vehicle they saw a red Ford Fiesta being driven erratically and jump a red light. At last their day appeared to be livening up! They gave chase and stopped the vehicle further along the M25.

PC Forsyth got out and walked up to the driver, whereupon he returned grinning at PC Bluestone. "You'll never guess what, he's got his trousers undone. I can't keep a straight face." So PC Bluestone went over to the driver and spoke to him, eventually issuing him with a fixed penalty ticket. PC Bluestone cautioned him and noted his reply verbatim which the offender signed; 'I had a hernia operation last Saturday and they had to shave my pubic hair which is now growing back with extreme irritation. I looked and didn't see any other cars coming.'

Man telephoned Chepstow police station to say that whilst digging in the garden he had found a quantity of bone, a shoe and a gnome. He was of the opinion that the bones may be human.

Teleprinter message...
Theft - MO: 'Woman went behind public house and whilst engaged in urinating in the squat position a man went to her and wrenched her handbag from her wrist.'

I recently had to charge a man who had been driving his car in a very drunken condition. When I asked him if he wished to make a reply to the charge he said, "Officer, it's all been a dreadful mistake. I got the amount you are allowed to drink before driving confused with the amount you are allowed to bring in through customs."

When the police surgeon took a blood sample for analysis the doctor said he was having difficulty understanding him because of the effects of the drink. The man then said, "Perhaps you had better come back when you're sober then."

More USA Court transcripts...

Question: "So, after the anaesthesia, when you came out of it, what did you observe with respect to your scalp?"
Answer: "I didn't see my scalp the whole time I was in hospital."
Question: "It was covered?"
Answer: "Yes, bandaged."
Question: "Then later on, what did you see?"
Answer "I had a skin graft. My whole buttocks and leg were removed and put on the top of my head."

Question: "Could you see him from where you were standing?"
Witness: "I could see his head."
Question: "And where was his head?"
Witness: "Just above his shoulders."

Question: "What can you tell us about the truthfulness and veracity of this defendant?"
Answer: "Oh, she'll tell the truth. She said she'd kill that bastard - and she did!"

Question: "When he went, had you gone and had she, if she wanted to and were able, for the time being excluding all the restraints on her not to go, gone also, would he have brought you, meaning you and she with him to the station?"
Prosecution: "Objection! That question should be taken out and shot."

THE FUNNY SIDE OF THE LAW

Question: "Any suggestion as to what prevented this from being a murder trial instead of an attempted murder trial?"
Answer: "The victim lived."

Question: "Are you sexually active?"
Answer: "No. I just lie there."

Question: "Are you qualified to give a urine sample?"
Answer: "Yes, I have been since early childhood."

An emergency call was received, the location given being a well known lovers lane. The call was made by a female who sounded very distressed, so ambulance control also asked the police to attend.
The ambulance crew arrived first and were waved down by the lady. She looked extremely embarrassed and led the crew to her car. There, they found a man kneeling in the back of the car in a state of undress. He was unable to move as his back had locked.
Trying their best to maintain a professional air, the crew asked the lady how long he had been in that position. She told them about an hour, 45 minutes of which she had been pinned underneath him. She then asked the crew how long they would be as she was desperate to get home.
The crew explained that they had to wait for the police to arrive and at this the lady became furious, shouting,
"Why on earth did you have to call them?"
The crew assured her that she wasn't in any trouble but the lady replied..."I will be when they arrive. My husband's a police officer."

A few more from Law exam papers...

'The Jury, when they were originally used, consisted of 11 people dragged in off the streets.'

'Intellectuality is not my strong point.'

In 1957 I was a Sergeant in the Bournemouth Borough Police Force and was on patrol one afternoon with a Constable. An annoyed woman complained to us that a man had just indecently exposed himself to her from the doorway of a public convenience and then gone back into the building (which was immediately across the road from us) and was still there. Entering the toilets, we arrested the sole occupant and he was conveyed to the police station in one vehicle whilst the woman followed in another. At the station she was asked to make a statement identifying the offender. Came the reply, "I can't. I never saw his face." With no alternative, he was released without charge but, obviously misjudging his good fortune, he repeated the offence twenty-four hours later in exactly the same place. This time the victim, seemingly 'elevating her sights', could identify him and appropriate legal retribution followed.

'At 7:55pm on 4 March 1981 taxi driver, Mr C. attended at the police station and saw Police Constable B. He said that he had a man in his taxi wishing to go to Russia and that he had been driving him around Birmingham for some time.' (It was established that the passenger was a day patient at a local mental hospital).

"We also do aromatherapy and acupuncture."

This one was taken from a Sunday Telegraph report of 27.9.92 which stated, 'Armed Chinese Communists held Hong Kong police at gunpoint on their boat and rubbed them.'

THE FUNNY SIDE OF THE LAW

This is the third title in the 'Funny Side' series. Copies of the previous two; 'The Funny Side of Teaching' and 'The Funny Side of Nursing' were offered as prizes in a national competition set by the Daily Mirror. Readers were asked to send in their funny stories relating to schools or hospitals. The following represents a selection from the winners entries...

My mother told me that on my return from my first visit to Sunday School she asked; "What did they talk about today?"
I replied, "Someone called Jesus Price".

My daughter is dyslexic. When she was about 11 years old she wrote in her history book; 'Mary Queen of Scots was a devout Alcoholic.' We assume she meant Catholic.

Dear Sir,
Dean can not do P.E. today because he has lost his sorts.

Dear P.E. Teacher,
Please make Rachel run fast and jump about today.

Dear Sir,
My son will not be able to do P.E. today because he has a mygrade.

Dear Sir,
Please excuse my son for not doing P.E. because he's got a saw leg.

THE FUNNY SIDE OF THE LAW

For our school magazine one pupil wrote;
'Mrs Gadd enjoys sinning in the choir'.

When I was taking the children to school on the school coach I asked them what they had had for breakfast. One little six year old raised her hand and called out, "I had strangled eggs on toast".

The young teacher in my Grandchildren's class was explaining the mysteries of outer space and, for example, pointed out COMET, which she described as a star with a tail. Asking the class if they knew of anything similar, one bright little girl offered, "Mickey Mouse."

THE FUNNY SIDE OF THE LAW

More from the Daily Mirror competition...

From young girls class book: 'A widow is a woman who marries a dead man."

My niece wrote: 'Jesus's birth was called the Immaculate Deception.'

"I'm a little shaver."

It was obvious that my four year old daughter, Grace, and her best friend, Jane, had fallen out and that they had had a fight at school. There was a slight scratch on Grace's cheek. The disagreement was over and when I asked her why there was blood on her face she made every effort to protect her friend and answered, "I cut myself shaving."

When I was teaching I once received a letter from a parent which read...
'My son came home from school yesterday with a hole in his new trousers. Will you please look into it?'

My wife teaches in a reception class of a primary school that has recently undergone a school inspection. During the visit one of the team quietly walked into my wife's classroom and sat down with his clipboard. One little girl asked him, "Can you write?"
"Yes, I can" he proudly answered.
"Then you should be sitting with the children on that table over there."

As a senior nurse I was observing a new member of staff applying treatment in the form of liquid nitrogen to a 'man's best friend' by means of a cotton wool swab. She asked nonchalantly, "Do you shake it before you use it?"
The question was aimed at me, referring to the excess treatment from the swab. I glanced at the embarrassed patient before we both burst out laughing.

Someone I know is a French Polisher by trade. He was admitted to hospital and, upon arrival, was asked the usual questions; religion, marital status, name of G.P. and so on. But when asked what colour his stools were he replied, "Mahogany."

My youngest granddaughter flew into the sitting room announcing that she'd had sex education at school. My two older granddaughters looked disinterested and said, "We know all about that. We learnt about it ages ago."
*She looked sympathetically at her dad and said, "Did you have to do that **three** times?"*

Also available

First published in 1995. Now in its third reprint The Funny Side of Teaching is a truly classic collection of anecdotes, misprints, misquotes and exam howlers from Britain's classrooms.

A 10% donation is made to **COMIC RELIEF** from every copy sold.

Still only £4.99

ISBN 0 9526395 0 5

The follow up. Published in 1996, The Funny Side of Nursing is a compilation of hysterical 'boobs' from nurses, doctors and ambulance crews. Bound to have you in stitches!

A 10% donation is made to **COMIC RELIEF** from every copy sold.

Still only £4.99

ISBN 0 9526395 2 1

These can be ordered from all good book shops if not currently in stock.

Acknowledgements

Special thanks are due to the following:

Contributors

Jonathan Ames, Karl Bluestone, Billboard, Blueprint,
L. Buckingham, Vera English, D. Evans, Clare Farrow,
Richard Ford, Fraggle Rock, T. Frost, Dave Glanvill,
Brian Hamilton, Alan Hancock, Lesley Hockin,
John Holborn, Sean Howe, Les Jeffries, C. Lovett,
M. Madden, Ted Marth, John May, Shaun McElheron,
W. Murphy, John Nelson, Steve Pailes, D.G. Phillips,
Police Review, Gillian Radcliffe, Denise Reece,
John Rusling, C. Satterthwaite, J. Shell, D. Slade,
Tony Slattery, The Law Society's Gazette, R. Thompson,
Daimon Tilley, P. Varrakalion, J. Walton, Martin Warnes,
Ann Williams, Roger Wilson, Belinda Young
... and The Daily Mirror.

Cartoonists

**Paul Cemmick, Allan Davies, Noel Ford,
Martin Honeysett, Larry, Fran Orford,
Ken Pyne, Colin Taylor, Nigel Thomas,
Geoff Thompson, Pete Williams.**

Cover illustration by John Richardson
Richardson Studios, Cleveland Lodge,
45 Cleveland Terrace, Darlington DL3 7HD.